WITNESS TO HISTORY

THE REMARKABLE UNTOLD STORY OF VIRGINIA CITY & NEVADA CITY MONTANA

AND HOW THEY CAME TO BE RESTORED AND SAVED FOR FUTURE GENERATIONS

JOHN D. ELLINGSEN

MF

MONTANA HISTORY

F O U N D A T I O N

sweetgrassbooks
a division of Farcountry Press

SOFTCOVER VERSION:
ISBN 10: 1-59152-089-4
ISBN 13: 978-1-59152-089-4

HARDCOVER VERSION:
ISBN 10: 1-59152-090-8
ISBN 13: 978-1-59152-090-0

Published by Montana History Foundation

For more information, write Montana History Foundation, 1750 North Washington Street, Helena, MT 59601 (406) 449-3770; www.mthistory.org

Produced by Sweetgrass; PO Box 5630, Helena, MT 59604 (800) 821-3874; www.sweetgrassbooks.com

You may order extra copies of this book by calling Farcountry Press toll free at (800) 821-3874.

The views expressed by the author/publisher in this book do not necessarily represent the views of, nor should be attributed to, Sweetgrass Books. Sweetgrass Books is not responsible for the content of the author/publisher's work.

Designed by Bruce Capdeville, Real World Design, Helena, MT

Printed in the United States.

15   14   13   12   11   1   2   3   4   5   6   7

To Charles Argalis Bovey and Sue Ford Bovey

FOREWORD

Sometimes the most remarkable and gifted individuals are the ones who call the least amount of attention to themselves. John Ellingsen is such an individual. With humility, and with a profound sense of commitment, he has dedicated his life to the restoration and preservation of Virginia City and Nevada City, Montana. The vision that Charlie Bovey first had for those places, John Ellingsen lovingly upholds.

John is not one for the spotlight, but his knowledge and passion were noticed by a philanthropist who recognized in John the treasure he is. She asked the Montana History Foundation to help get his stories preserved and published. Her vision and John's life are at the heart of this book.

This is our attempt to honor a donor and honor John, all for the benefit of Montana's history. We hope in reading this book you will be able to say we accomplished our goal.

–Amy Sullivan, Executive Director,
Montana History Foundation, October 2011

EDITOR'S PREFACE

It has been a privilege for me to work with and get to know John Ellingsen over the past two years. During that time I made many trips to Virginia City and Nevada City. When the fickle mountain weather permitted, we would walk the streets while he told me the history of nearly every structure we passed. Other times we would sit at his house in Nevada City, or on the porch at The Bennett House, poring over old photos and drawings. As I listened to his stories of buildings and people in Alder Gulch over the last century and a half, I began to absorb his enthusiasm for a place that represents a pivotal part of the history of the American West. I also learned much about John's own story: about his association with the remarkable Charlie Bovey; about the circumstances that brought John here; about the lessons he learned here; and about the choices he made that kept him here.

Working with John posed two big challenges. The first was to help him take the enormous amount of material he has documented and written and choose a small amount that we could shape into the present book. It is John's hope, and mine, that this volume will serve to whet the appetite of the reader and lead him or her to the rich vein of writing on this important part of the history of Montana and the West.

The second challenge I faced was how to persuade John to overcome his modesty and write about himself and his own life. His perspective is a unique one, and we who care about the history of the West are fortunate that John Ellingsen is willing to share his knowledge, insight, and passion with us.

–Clay Scott

ACKNOWLEDGEMENTS

I am indebted to scores of individuals and organizations—more than I can possibly name here. But I would be remiss in not thanking the Montana History Foundation, for their support of historically important projects around Montana, as well as their support of my own research and writing; the Montana Preservation Alliance, for their vital work in Virginia City and elsewhere in our state; the National Trust for Historic Preservation, for their critical role in saving Virginia and Nevada Cities; John and Bernice De Haas, who helped me understand why historic preservation matters, and who encouraged me to devote my life to that pursuit; and Charles, Sue, and Ford Bovey, who gave me the opportunity to carry out meaningful work in a place like no other.

–John D. Ellingsen

This is a book about Virginia City and Nevada City, Montana, past and present. It is not in any way intended to be the definitive history of these two wonderful and important communities, although I am currently at work on an in-depth study, which I hope to publish at a later date.

I have several motives in writing the present volume. Firstly, I would like to offer the reader a sort of sampler or brief sketch of the history of Virginia City and Nevada City, from their origins to the present day. It is my hope that the reader will be enticed to read further, for many fine books, essays, and articles have been written about the mining communities of Alder Gulch and southwest Montana. Some have been serious historical works, and some have attempted to re-create the feel of life here during the gold rush.

As I have said, I myself am collecting material for two detailed studies—building by building—of both Virginia and Nevada Cities. With the present volume, however, my aim is somewhat different. True, you will find in these pages historical information, descriptions, and histories of particular buildings, and anecdotes from those frenzied early years when the Gulch was settled. But I believe I have something else to offer, and that is a unique perspective on how it is that these wonderful places still exist today.

 The author on an early visit to Virginia City

It might be easy for the casual visitor to assume that these old buildings were always here and that they were always so well preserved. But how is it that today's Virginia City—one of the true treasures of the West—survived the fate of attrition, neglect, and destruction that befell so many other Montana mining towns? How did Nevada City come to exist? And how did these wonderful streets and buildings, in which our history lives and breathes, come under the protection of the State of Montana so that they may be enjoyed by future generations instead of being dismantled for firewood or sold piecemeal to the highest bidder?

The answer to those questions, I believe, forms the outlines of one of the most significant stories of historic preservation in the western United States, a story at the center of which is the remarkable and visionary Charlie Bovey. He was an important mentor to me and an inspiration. In the following pages, I'd like to add my perspective to what has been largely an untold story—that of Charlie's

crucial role in making these places what they are today. My own association with Charlie Bovey was a long and fruitful one, and I feel privileged to have had the chance to learn from him and work with him in a modest way to help make the communities of Alder Gulch what they are today. Without Charlie's vision—at a time when many people thought his ideas eccentric—it is possible that very few of the historic buildings of the Gulch would be standing today.

Charlie and Sue Bovey may have been pioneers, but they weren't alone. And so the story of Virginia City and Nevada City is also the story of the efforts of a host of passionate individuals and committed organizations, from Montana and around the country, to preserve something that they recognized as valuable. And it is a small part of the big story about why history matters and why the preservation of the material culture of a bygone era can be such an important window to understanding who we are today.

THE EARLY DAYS OF VIRGINIA CITY

A VERY BRIEF HISTORY OF THAT TUMULTUOUS PERIOD
LEADING UP TO THE DISCOVERY OF GOLD IN ALDER GULCH

There is a magic to Virginia City. I felt it on my first visit here as a child, and I've never ceased to feel it. Part of my motivation in writing this little book is to try and convey some of that to my reader. Not by romanticizing this place or any particular era of its history, but simply by trying to explain some of what I feel when I walk these streets that I know so well. But in order to appreciate and understand Virginia City, we're first going to have to go back a bit, to the time before gold was discovered here.

I suppose that, since you are reading a book about Virginia City, you are probably also fascinated by the history of early Montana and the American West in general. I know I am. I have always been drawn to that period of western history in the mid-to-late 1800s, a time when our nation was reinventing and redefining itself. In the American West at that time, life was unpredictable, frequently dangerous, and often exhilarating. It was a time when old customs clashed with new ideas, while technology was changing almost as rapidly as it is today: the telegraph competed with old-fashioned letters, breech-loading firearms had rendered muzzleloaders obsolete, and steamboats and wagons were giving way to the railroad. All this was happening before, during, and after the American Civil War. Many Americans were uneasy and frightened by the pace of change, and by the national upheaval. But many others embraced the idea that anything was possible, the idea that—no matter his background—a person could re-create himself. And for thousands of Americans, that meant heading west, into the unknown, into the land of infinite possibility.

 Henry Edgar in his later years

Many of the settlers were drawn west in the hopes of finding "empty" land where they could farm and ranch. (Of course, the idea that there were indigenous inhabitants of the territories in question, and that they might have a claim to the land, was something that never occurred to most of the land-hungry settlers.)

At the same time, adding to the frenzied and chaotic pace of westward expansion, gold was being discovered throughout the West—in California, and in what would become the states of Oregon, Colorado, Washington, Utah, and Idaho. On July 28, 1862, prospectors found gold in Grasshopper Creek, at the site of present-day Bannack, Montana. That was not the first time gold had been found in what was soon to be Montana Territory, but Bannack was the earliest significant discovery of gold here. It was the first real indication that the precious yellow metal was present in Montana in important quantities. Within months, the population of Bannack had grown to about 1,000 inhabitants.

By now, lured by the prospect of a quick fortune—which, sadly, would not materialize for most—miners, would-be miners, entrepreneurs, and fortune seekers (not to mention deserters, ladies "of ill repute," card sharks, confidence men, and road agents) were streaming into the area. Bannack was already losing interest for the more intrepid of the prospectors, who began to search farther afield in the hopes of finding their own claim. Such individuals were Henry Edgar of Scotland, Barney Hughes of Ireland, and Ohioan Tom Cover, along with three men from New Brunswick: James (Bill) Sweeney, Bill Fairweather, and Harry Rodgers. Together they had attempted to prospect along the Yellowstone River, but were turned back by Crow Indians. They headed back toward Bannack, intending to restock their supplies and try again. They had made their way down the Madison Valley and up over the saddle connecting the Tobacco Root Mountains to the Gravelly Range. It was late in the day on May 26, 1863, when the party arrived at what seemed like as good a campsite as any. They were at nearly

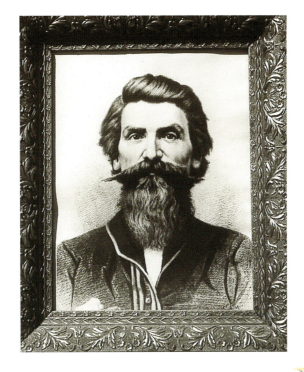

 Bill Fairweather, discoverer of gold in Alder Gulch

6,000 feet elevation, toward the top of a pine and fir and sagebrush covered bowl. They picketed the horses near a narrow, rushing stream choked with alders. With plenty of light left before sunset, the men began looking around, and some promising rock formations caught their attention. Out of habit, they got out their prospecting tools and immediately found "colors" of gold. By the end of that first evening, they realized already that they had made a significant strike.

Two days later, they staked out their claims along the stream bank—100 feet per claim—then hurried back to Bannack for supplies. If the six men had hoped to keep their discovery a secret, it was a vain hope. This is an entry in Henry Edgar's diary:

"…I was sitting in a saloon, talking with some friends; there were lots of men that were strangers to me; they were telling that we brought in a horse-load of gold and not one of the party had told that we had brought in a color…Well, we have been feasted and cared for like princes…"

May 26, 1863: gold is discovered in Alder Gulch.

The rumor of the party's strike spread quickly, and as they attempted to sneak out of Bannack early the next morning to return to their claims, they found themselves followed by at least 200 men. Realizing they could not shake the crowd of gold-hungry prospectors, Egdar made a clean breast of the matter and told the crowd that they had found $189 worth of gold in a matter of hours. That got everyone's attention. Then he went on to say that his party had already staked their claims, and that those claims were legally binding and must be respected. After talking it over for a while, the crowd agreed. Out of that discussion arose a set of guidelines that evolved into the laws that would eventually govern the communities of Alder Gulch. It seems remarkable that this group of miners and fortune seekers, living in a lawless territory, recognized so early on the need for structure, organization, and rules. In the absence of those things, they understood, chaos would ensue, which would be to the detriment of the fortunes of all of them. They arrived at the site that would become Virginia City on June 6, 1863. Almost immediately, the entire gulch was staked out.

Within days, many more prospectors followed the original group, and there were soon hundreds of tents and lean-tos up and down a 14-mile stretch of Alder Gulch. Those makeshift camps soon grew into rough shacks and log cabins and then permanent communities. The largest of these communities, and by far the most important, was Virginia City—a place to which I have devoted nearly my entire adult life.

A ROUGH BEGINNING

A BRIEF DESCRIPTION OF LIFE IN THE FIRST MONTHS
OF THE ALDER GULCH SETTLEMENTS, DURING WHICH

A NOTORIOUS GANG OF OUTLAWS MET WITH ROUGH JUSTICE,
ORDER EMERGED FROM LAWLESSNESS, AND
VIRGINIA CITY WENT FROM TENT CITY TO TERRITORIAL CAPITAL

The landscape of the American West is dotted with the skeletons of once-bustling towns that were born during the gold rush years of the second half of the 1800s. Most of these places had an ephemeral life and are now completely abandoned. In some of them, dilapidated buildings are still standing. In others, you have to look hard to discover traces of previous occupation.

You might find a brass doorknob among a pile of rocks, or the remnants of a stone foundation almost hidden in the grass, or a piece of some rusted implement whose original use is not always easy to determine. More often the tailings and tailrace are all that is left—old scars that will be visible for many decades more before they too melt back into the landscape. But some of these old settlements survived—and some even thrived—making the transition into the post-mining era. Helena, Montana, is, of course, one prime example. And another—although their histories are quite different—is Helena's predecessor and old rival, Virginia City.

Virginia City, to me, is a place like no other. I was smitten with it the first time I came here as a child, and I still am to this day. I would give anything to have been able to walk its streets a century and a half ago. I have had people tell me that I romanticize the past. I don't think that is exactly true. I certainly don't believe, for example, that life in Virginia City at the height of the gold rush, and in the following years, was perfect. Daily existence was difficult—probably more so than we can imagine. Material comforts were few. Many people must have felt lonely and isolated. Some didn't live long. Most probably got by with a less-than-nutritious diet. Above all, I don't believe that most

A mule team on Van Buren Street, 1860s

must have been a real excitement in the air. At the beginning, of course, that excitement was due almost entirely to the gold that defined what Alder Gulch was all about. It was the biggest placer gold discovery in Montana, and some say the biggest the world has ever known. Alder Gulch ultimately yielded over $100 million in gold (at $16 an ounce.) In 2011, that amount would be well in excess of a billion dollars. With the "smell" of so much wealth in the air, those early weeks and months must have been frenzied up and down the Gulch. Frenzied, but not completely out of control.

By June 16, 1863 (a mere three weeks after the Fairweather party had made its discovery), Virginia City had already been organized. By that I mean that it was planned and platted as a permanent city from the very beginning, with straight streets and square corners. The Verona Town Company filed claim on a 320-acre piece of land to be used as a town site. The proposed name for the new town was Varina, after the wife of Jefferson Davis—then the president of the Confederate States of America. Dr. Gaylord Bissell, who had been elected judge of the Fairweather Mining District,

people today understand how dull and routine much of life was during that period. Basic, necessary chores were a real burden: chores such as carrying water, chopping wood, gathering food, cooking, washing, dealing with sewage. Nothing was done with the flip of a switch or the pull of a lever. So no, I don't romanticize life then. But I do feel that it is important to try and reach across the decades and centuries, and to use our imagination to try and understand people who in almost every fundamental way were just like us.

So…what was life really like in Alder Gulch in those early days and months? Well, for one thing (and, yes, I am aware that I am contradicting what I just said about much of life being dull), there and whose sympathies lay with the Unionists, crossed out the word Varina on the charter that was presented to him and replaced it with Virginia, which was to become the name of the city. Although many of the new residents of the area had come west to escape the war that was ravaging "The States," tensions remained high for many years in Alder Gulch between Union and Confederate sympathizers.

It is fortunate that some of those early residents had the foresight to plan Virginia City so carefully. Even they could not have foreseen how quickly the communities of Alder Gulch would grow. By fall of that first year, Virginia City proper had an estimated 10,000 inhabitants. The whole district (the so-called 14-Mile City), including the towns of Summit, Highland, Pine Grove, Central City, Nevada City, Adobetown, and Junction, is thought to have had a population of around 35,000.

But who were these people? Well, for one thing, they were not all miners. After some time had passed and the population ballooned, the character of Virginia City must have changed markedly.

MECHANICAL BAKERY

This log structure (on the left in this photo) was the very first house built in Virginia City, a fact confirmed by Thomas Dimsdale when he wrote his "Vigilantes of Montana" in 1865. Numerous other writers have since referred to it as Virginia City's first building, among them C. Hedges in his historical address on the dedication of the new courthouse on July 4, 1876.

The Mechanical Bakery was built in early June 1863, by T. C. Luce, who had previously operated a cracker bakery in Denver. His ambition of installing machinery in his Virginia City establishment was never realized, and Luce evidently later moved to Cover Street. The building subsequently became a residential dwelling and remained so until it was acquired by Charlie Bovey, at which point it became part of the Bale of Hay Saloon.

The Masons played a crucial role in the development of Virginia City.

It wasn't long before the men who made their living directly from gold were in the minority. A small number of these miners made fortunes beyond their wildest dreams. Quite a few managed to get together enough money to buy a piece of land, or start a business somewhere, or go back east and live modestly off their savings. The vast majority of the miners, however, made very little money and tended to squander what they did make.

As for the rest of the population of Alder Gulch, it was a diverse mix. There were merchants, carpenters, stonemasons, and men of the cloth. There were blacksmiths, millers, printers, teachers, performers, and butchers. There were fraternal organizations, chief among them the Masons, that played a crucial role in the development of Virginia City. There were chefs who served haute cuisine.

There were teachers of French and Latin, dance instructors, boxing coaches, and professional theatre troupes. And there were people who provided every manner of service—both licit and illicit.

The majority of these people were single American men of European descent (including hundreds of former soldiers—most of whom had probably not been "honorably discharged" from their service), but there were also families and single women. And the communities of Alder Gulch displayed a surprising ethnic diversity as well. A not inconsiderable number of African Americans established themselves in and around Virginia City. There were Canadians (like Bill Fairweather), Mexicans, South Americans, and representatives of several European countries. And, from early on, there was a very significant Chinese presence.

I would like to say a few words about this very important segment of the population of Alder Gulch.

The greatest number of the Chinese in Montana had been laborers, working to build the Central Pacific Railroad from California eastward. When that monumental task was finally completed and the rails from east and west were joined in northern Utah in 1869, the Chinese laborers found themselves out of work. Many of them headed north to Virginia City; the Chinese community soon numbered as many as 500 souls. The Chinese were not only miners—they found work as cooks, woodcutters, waiters, and of course, laundrymen. It was the identification of the Chinese with the latter occupation that made them targets of a discriminatory tax. Montana's second Territorial Legislature, in 1867, enacted a tax of $10 per quarter (a substantial amount of money) on all males "who now or who may hereafter be engaged in the laundry business." That amount was later upped to $15 per quarter, and then $20. The tax was eventually repealed. The Chinese managed, despite considerable prejudice, to thrive here, often diligently working claims abandoned by the first impatient wave of miners. They lived in a Chinatown in Virginia City and had their own shops, temples, and restaurants. Through their hard work and honesty, they eventually won a grudging respect from the non-Chinese inhabitants of Alder Gulch.

 The Chinese community in Virginia City numbered as many as 500.

Stages connected Virginia City with the rest of the world.

All things considered, Virginia City made an almost inconceivably smooth transition from a chaotic camp of lean-tos, mud huts, and wickiups to a well-organized, well-planned, well-run town. It was a smooth transition, but with one major bump in the road.

It goes without saying that wherever money is being made in great quantities, violence and crime arc not far behind. It should come as no great surprise, therefore, that criminals, robbers, hoodlums, petty thieves, murderers, pickpockets, professional gamblers, river pirates, swindlers, confidence tricksters, and the like arrived in Alder Gulch almost with the very first wave of gold

seekers. They came from the gold camps of Nevada, California, Washington, and Oregon, or up the Missouri River by steamboat via Fort Benton, or from Salt Lake City.

This plague of crime was of a sort that virtually all gold mining communities throughout the West had to deal with. But in Alder Gulch, and elsewhere in what was to become Montana Territory, the wave of violence reached epidemic proportions. The "road agents" concentrated in particular on the 60-mile road between Virginia City and Bannack, on the trail that led north toward Fort Benton (the terminus of the steamboat route up the Missouri River), and on the route that went south toward Salt Lake City. It was a while before proper and secure banks could be established in Virginia City, and most miners tried to get their hard-earned gold out of Montana on their own persons. But a string of robberies, many of them culminating in murder, must have made the inhabitants of Alder Gulch and Bannack feel like they were under siege. Men were beaten and robbed and intimidated and murdered. Some of the men who carried out these crimes were acting alone, or in twos and threes. But by far the majority of the violent crime appears to have been committed by larger groups. And one such group was so well organized, so well informed and so well connected, that it seemed to be almost more of a mafia than a gang.

Here is where we must speak of that brief but violent page of the history of early Montana that was defined by the gang in question and its demise at the hands of the Vigilantes. And here, also, is where a bit of controversy enters the picture. Not only is there disagreement on the details of this chapter—among contemporary witnesses as well as modern historians—but there also is disagreement on some of the basic elements of the story. The most fundamental questions, of course, regard the Vigilantes and whether or not their actions were justified, as well as the leadership of the gang and the guilt or innocence of Henry Plummer.

Before I go any further, I would like to say that I've always felt that the Vigilante story has been overemphasized to the extent that it detracts somewhat from the study of other aspects of life in the early history of Montana. Having said that, I must admit that I understand why the story—whatever interpretation you prefer—is undeniably dramatic. Many of us (and I am sometimes guilty of this) want the past to conform to our images of it. And the images most of us have of the American West are so deeply ingrained in us that, in a place like Virginia City, we tend to look for them everywhere and in everything. Most of these images, of course, are the creation of Hollywood imaginations and bear little or no resemblance to historical reality. Even the "true" elements of a Hollywood Western tend to be so jumbled up, chronologically askew, and out of context as to be fairly meaningless. Be that as it may, the chapter of Virginia City's history that witnessed the Vigilantes and the gang of road agents was more dramatic, more "western," than any Hollywood screenwriter could have dreamed up. Many fine writers and historians have dealt with this subject, but I feel compelled to devote a few words here to this tale of violence, greed, and frontier justice.

Henry Plummer was a larger-than-life character known as much for his charm, good looks, and powers of persuasion as for his violent temper. He was born in Maine, but made his way as a young man to the gold fields of California. He thrived there, made money, invested in business, and seems generally to have been well liked and respected. At the age of only 24, he was elected sheriff of Nevada City, California. Shortly afterward, Plummer killed a man with whose wife he had been having an affair—not the only time in his life he would kill someone over a dispute about a woman. He was sentenced to ten years in prison for that first murder, but was pardoned after serving only six months. He eventually made his way to Bannack (in what was then Idaho Territory) and was elected sheriff of that town as well, his history of violence and his prison record notwithstanding. By then (according to some accounts), Plummer was committed to a life of crime, for which, as sheriff, he would have been perfectly situated. He gathered together a collection of tough characters, some of whom he had known in prison. (In fact, it was the support of these men that probably helped him become elected sheriff.)

At this time, there was a very active and effective criminal gang who called themselves "The Innocents" (their intentionally ironic password was "I am innocent"). It has long been assumed (though it is now disputed) that Sheriff Henry Plummer was in effect the leader of the gang. Whether or not he was, the gang seems to have infiltrated and controlled virtually everything in Bannack. When gold was discovered 60 miles away in Alder Gulch, and with traffic increasing between the two mining settlements, The Innocents saw the promise of easy pickings and went to work in earnest. This was not merely a band of thugs, but a well-structured criminal organization with extraordinary connections and a highly developed system of communications. Any time there was to be a shipment of gold or other valuables, it seems, the gang learned of it. With the law-abiding inhabitants offering little real resistance, The Innocents grew bolder and bolder, plundering almost at will. Especially susceptible to foul play were the small parties or individual

WM. KISKADDEN & CO. (THE VIGILANTE BARN)

This was Virginia City's first stone building, constructed in the summer of 1863. Its popular name—"The Vigilante Barn"—reflects its most prominent role as the place where the Vigilantes signed their oath. Or did they?

There is now a fair amount of disagreement about whether the Vigilantes actually held their first meeting here or elsewhere. There are other locations that would like to claim that honor. It seems plausible, in this case, that the Vigilantes held a series of secretive meetings, possibly in a variety of locations, leading up to the signing of their oath, which may (or may not) have taken place at the Vigilante Barn.

Be that as it may, the building was at that time occupied by William Kiskadden & Co., and divided into three stores, with French doors opening into the street.

The eastern two-thirds of the building was occupied from September 5, 1864, to March 18, 1865, by Baum, Angevine and Merry, while Taylor, Thompson & Co. did business out of the western third. Gorham & Patton, grocers, moved their premises to the eastern

third in March 1865, while the western part still operated under the name of The San Francisco Meat Market.

Today, when we stand and study the stone and timbers that have stood for a century and a half, it is hard not to be taken back to that tumultuous and confusing and exhilarating time in our history. As for whether the building really played the role attributed to it, we'll never know for certain. Popular history likes to simplify events, and, of course, real life does not always provide us with a neat narrative!

We the undersigned uniting cursive in a party for the laudible purpos of arresting thiers & mrderers & recover stollen propperty do pledg ourselvs as our sacred honor each to all others & solemnly swear that we will reveal no secrets violate no laws of right & never desert eachother or our standerd of justice. So help us God. as witnel our hand & seal this 23 of December A D 1863

The Vigilante oath

miners, cocky or confident enough to believe they could make it to safety with their earnings. Such individuals died by the dozens. During the summer and fall of 1863, The Innocents are believed to have been responsible for upwards of 100 murders in what is now southwest Montana. The gang is also thought to have stolen around $250,000 worth of gold. The situation persisted through the fall and into December. It is easy for us in hindsight to believe we would have resisted, but the (non-criminal) inhabitants of the Montana gold camps must have been paralyzed with fear during that period.

There came a point, however, at which enough was enough. In December 1863 a group of citizens from Nevada City arrested and tried George Ives for murder. He was hanged on December 21, and a few days later, a group of men calling themselves the Vigilance Committee formed in Virginia City. The "Vigilantes" set out to capture and "administer justice" to as many road agents as they could. In the course of less than a month, 22 suspected gang members were hanged. One of the men they captured accused Henry Plummer of being the leader of the gang, so Plummer was caught and hanged as well.

Today, it is far from clear whether the Vigilantes should be viewed as frontier heroes, doing what needed to be done to fight violent criminals, or whether they were themselves outlaws, lynching without trial men who may have been innocent. But whatever you believe, and whether or not Henry Plummer was ultimately involved with The Innocents, the actions of the Vigilantes did effectively put an end to the rash of robberies and murders that had plagued the Montana gold settlements, and ushered in a more peaceful era. It was an era in which culture blossomed, commerce flourished, and law and order began to prevail. And these elements set the scene for Virginia City's dramatic and improbable transition from mining camp to territorial capital.

THE GLORY DAYS OF VIRGINIA CITY

A HASTY CHRONOLOGY OF THOSE YEARS IN WHICH
MONTANA BECAME A TERRITORY,

AND VIRGINIA CITY BRIEFLY ITS CAPITAL

As I mentioned earlier, the people flooding into Virginia City were not all necessarily seeking gold. A large percentage of them were merchants of one kind or another; many were emigrants who, deciding the West Coast was too far, had veered off the Oregon Trail toward southwest Montana; and many—perhaps most—were simply afflicted with the restlessness that was common to so many Americans during that period.

There were several main routes by which these immigrants came to Virginia City. From the east, from what is now Casper, Wyoming, north to the Bozeman Trail and then west; from the west (mostly California), via either Corinne, Utah, or overland from Walla Walla, Washington; and from the north, up the Missouri River via steamboat to Fort Benton and south to Virginia City from there. Steamboat traffic was very significant for a period of several years, although it was seasonal: Much of the river was frozen in the winter, and the water flows were low late in the summer. Many of the artifacts presently in Virginia City were brought up the Missouri River. Steamboat traffic eventually petered out for two main reasons: Firstly, a larger U.S. Army presence rendered the area of present-day Montana and Wyoming much safer (from a non-Indian point of view), and so more people were tempted to travel overland; and secondly, the transcontinental railroad was finally completed, making it easier, cheaper, and safer to transport people and goods north from Utah.

People and mail at this time were transported into Virginia City primarily via horses, light coaches, and wagons. Heavier freight was brought in on sturdy wagons, pulled by either oxen or mule teams. There was for some time a type of "pony express"

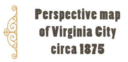

Perspective map of Virginia City circa 1875

route between Fort Bridger, in Utah Territory and Bannack. Stagecoach service soon began as well, linking Virginia City and Bannack to both Fort Benton to the north and Salt Lake City to the south. It was the development of safe and efficient transportation routes, more than perhaps any other factor, that created the conditions necessary for Virginia City to evolve into the important center of culture, commerce, and politics it was to become.

The interior West—in particular, what are now the states of Montana, Idaho, and Washington—was not a high priority of America's leaders until the 1860s. With the discovery of significant quantities of gold throughout the West, however, the folks on Capitol Hill began to give a little more thought to the settling and organizing of this part of the country. Today's western Montana (west of the Continental Divide) became part of Washington Territory in 1854. The eastern part of today's Montana became, in 1861, part of Dakota Territory. The proliferation of gold strikes in what is now Idaho and Montana gave impetus to the creation of Idaho Territory (which included Montana)

The excitement of the gold rush in Virginia City – a rare early photograph

in March 1863. Only two months later, the discovery of gold by Bill Fairweather and his party in Alder Gulch gave rise to the suggestion that yet another territory might be created: one that would split off from Idaho. That suggestion took hold with Sidney Edgerton, who had just arrived in the West to fill his appointment as chief justice of Idaho Territory. As Virginia City began to grow in size and importance, more and more voices were raised in favor of creating a new territory east of the Continental Divide. One of the leaders of this movement was Wilbur Sanders. Sanders helped raise the money to send Edgerton to Washington, D.C. as a representative. The majority of the inhabitants of Bannack and Virginia City, to the extent that they had any party affiliation, were Democrats, and some of them protested the selection of Edgerton, a Republican. But Sanders made the argument that a Republican would have greater influence with the current Republican administration, which proved indeed to be the case. After some wrangling and political

McGOVERN'S DRY GOODS STORE

This wonderful building occupies a unique place in historical restoration. Not only is it an original building, but its interior furnishings and stock are exactly as they were left by the last owners, Hanna and Mary McGovern, when they hung up the OUT TO LUNCH sign in the 1930s, never to take it down again.

The building was owned by a Mr. James Sheehan, who sold it in June 1864 to Messrs. William Kastor, B. Berry, S. H. Bowman, and G. Goldberg. Kastor operated it for a few months as The Pioneer Store, selling clothing, before moving across the street. At that point, his partner, Goldberg, took it over. If you study the front of the building very closely, you can still make out the words G. GOLDBERG above the French doors.

The "McGovern" building was converted to a residence around 1866. The single door to the west of the storefront was, at the time, called The Weston Hotel. The designation "hotel" probably implied a grandiosity that didn't exist. It consisted of four rooms, each 6 feet by 12 feet, and guests had to pass through one room to get to the next. There was also a large living room with a skylight in the center and a kitchen in the rear.

The building's next owner was Thomas Deyarmon, the founder of The Madisonian, who acquired it as a residential rental. Finally, the property ended up in the hands of Hanna and Mary McGovern, whose parents lived in the Star Bakery building in Nevada City. They had taken over Mrs. O. D. French's Dry Goods and Millinary Store, which was then located in the corner of Creighton's Stone Block, upon the demise of Mrs. French. In 1910, they moved the shop to its present location, where they continued into the 1930s. For many years the McGovern store, with its friendly bell on the door, was a favorite gathering place for the ladies of Alder Gulch.

A GOOD WOMAN IS HARD TO FIND

It's easy to forget that there were women in Alder Gulch—and lots of them. Many, of course, were "ladies of the night." (There were scores of euphemisms for prostitutes in use at that time, including "soiled doves," "prairie doves," "women of evil name and evil fame," "frail sisters," "scarlet ladies," "ladies of easy virtue," and "calico queens.") Then there were the "Hurdy Gurdy Girls," who, for a little bit of gold dust, would dance with a customer for five or ten minutes, sometimes dancing up to 50 times in the course of an evening!

The prostitutes were generally the first women to arrive at the gold camps of the West, and this was certainly the case in Alder Gulch. The stigma attached to this profession, while it certainly existed, was much less in a place like Virginia City than it was back in "civilization," and the lines were sometimes blurred between "professional" and "virtuous" women. Prostitutes were naturally in the business of making money, and many of them made a lot of it. Some of them invested their capital wisely, and many opened successful enterprises of various kinds. In the early days of Virginia City, where men with a little gold in their pockets were drunk on the possibility of making their fortune, an astute and disciplined businesswoman could do quite well.

Prostitutes who managed to do so were eventually accepted—more or less—into respectable society.

As for the "virtuous" women, there were at first very few of them in Alder Gulch, but they soon began to arrive, mostly in the company of their families. In some cases, they were seeking runaway husbands. In other cases, they arrived only to find that their husband had died, been killed, or had run off to yet another gold camp.

It was a hard life for these women, whether married, widowed, or abandoned, but they soon began to band together. The Montana Post, in the absence of much hard news, often mentioned in "society" columns which lady had drunk tea with whom. Many of these women had brought with them the attitudes and fashions of the East, and wore hoop skirts and fancy shoes and feathered hats, and carried parasols as they stepped along the less-than-genteel streets of Virginia City. As they did so, they no doubt encountered "soiled doves," in all probability dressed as finely as they. Did the women greet each other? Did the "good woman" acknowledge her "sister" at all? I would like to think that she did—if only with the tiniest nod of her head as they passed in the street.

THE HURDY-GURDY HOUSE, VIRGINIA, MONTANA.

maneuvering, the administration agreed to create the new territory. James Ashley, who was the head of the U.S. Committee on Territories, is credited with coming up with the name "Montana." (In fact, Ashley had attempted to give that name a year earlier to what became Idaho Territory.) On May 26, 1864 (exactly one year after the discovery of gold by the Fairweather party), President Abraham Lincoln signed Montana Territory into existence.

Sidney Edgerton was named governor of the new territory and returned to Montana. He assembled the first legislature in Bannack, and one of the first bills they enacted was to move the territorial capital to Virginia City. Edgerton didn't last long in office, and for reasons that are not completely understood, he left Montana in September 1865. A charismatic Irishman named Thomas Francis Meagher became acting governor and established his office in Virginia City near the corner of Van Buren and Wallace Streets. Territorial business had started to run fairly smoothly, but by 1870 the era of Virginia City's preeminence was already starting to wane. A serious movement arose—and rapidly gained momentum — to move Montana's capital yet again. This time, the focus was on the new and thriving settlement of Last Chance Gulch—soon to be known as Helena. Those in favor of keeping the capital in Virginia City won the political battle, but only temporarily. In 1874, the people of Montana voted again on the issue, and amid accusations of fraud and ballot box stuffing, the matter was sent to the courts. After an appeal to the U.S. Supreme Court, the case returned to the Montana court. Finally, Helena won out, spelling an end to the most glorious period in the history of Virginia City.

THE WEEKLY HERALD.

THE CAPITAL CASE.

Victory Over Fraud!

Acting-Governor Callaway Anticipates the Writ of Mandate.

And With United States Marshal Wheeler Meets and Canvasses the True Vote.

The Result Declared in Accordance Therewith, and the Proclamation Issued.

The Herald's Figures of Sept 1, 1874, Verified, and Helena is the Capital of Montana.

[SPECIAL TELEGRAMS TO THE HERALD.]
VIRGINIA CITY, M. T., January 11, 4 p. m.
Our hopes of anticipated obedience to the

 The Helena Weekly Herald, January 14, 1875

Virginia City schoolchildren, 1867

THE CALL OF THE PAST

HOW A MONTANA RANCH BOY LEARNED TO LOVE THE ARCHITECTURE
AND MATERIAL CULTURE OF THE EARLY AMERICAN WEST,

AND HOW HE SUBSEQUENTLY CAME TO DEVOTE HIS LIFE TO THE STUDY
AND PRESERVATION OF THE BUILDINGS OF THAT PERIOD

I've described the magnet that Virginia City was in the early days following the discovery of gold. People from all walks of life flocked here—citizens of many nations, members of many religious communities, men and women from every social class. They came to make money, of course, but they were also drawn by the excitement, by the electric atmosphere that must have characterized Alder Gulch during that period. Some, no doubt, also came here to reinvent or rediscover themselves, or to hide or lose themselves.

As for me, arriving here as I did a good century after the Fairweather discovery, I would say I came to Virginia City to find myself—or rather, to make a place for that part of myself that I had been in touch with since I was a child.

In many respects, I've always felt more at home in the past than in the present; I've felt that certain eras spoke to me. In particular, I've long been convinced that we Americans were in such a hurry to launch ourselves into the 20th century that we neglected much of what the 19th century had to teach us. Even as a child in Great Falls, I mourned the needless destruction of old buildings and felt uncomfortable with the assumption that modern was necessarily better. I felt the loss of the Victorian buildings that were thoughtlessly torn down as keenly as if they had been members of my own family.

I guess it's fair to say that, as a boy, I didn't like the modern world very much. Let me rephrase that: I didn't like what was modern, if what was understood by that term was an out-of-hand dismissal of what had gone before. And during my childhood, in the aftermath of WWII, I believe it is fair to say that many people did indeed define modern in that way. But for me, the past and

present have always run together in a continuum, and it has always struck me as artificial and simplistic to separate them so neatly. I also find there to be arrogance in the summary rejection of the past, because doing so implies that the era a person inhabits represents a kind of perfection.

I don't remember a single, specific event or moment in which my distrust of modernity, or my love of the past, was born. Rather, it was more of a cumulative series of impressions and observations. It happened at a time when a rampant wave of "modernizing" was sweeping through Great Falls. In fact, the post-war love of the modern bordered on an infatuation with the future. It was a mentality that believed the future held the key to happiness, and that in the future lay the solution to all of society's ills. The flip side of that mentality, of course, was the rejection of everything that was not seen as modern. The past was old-fashioned, irrelevant, and an impediment to Almighty Progress. Obviously, these attitudes were not unique to post-war America and certainly not unique to Great Falls. This type of wholesale rejection of the immediate past has occurred at

The following anecdote will give the reader some inkling how much I identified with and cared about old buildings. My mother and I were faithful members of the Methodist Church, housed in a lovely old building. But when, in 1952, the church was torn down so that something more modern could be built in its place, I refused to attend service there. Henceforth, respecting my wishes (and, I believe, sharing my sentiments), my mother took me to the Christian Church. In this case, architectural integrity trumped sectarian allegiance. I was clearly a preservationist even then.

different times and places throughout history. However, Great Falls, Montana, was my world. That is where I formed my first impressions of what it meant to be living in a rapidly changing world. That is where I first felt that we have an obligation to the past—not to worship it as perfect, but to respect it and learn from it. For by learning about our immediate past, we are, ultimately, learning valuable lessons about ourselves and about what it means to be a human being.

As a boy, naturally, I didn't formulate these thoughts in that way. I wasn't able to articulate my distress and feelings of hopelessness as our society so wantonly tossed aside things of artistry, craftsmanship, ingenuity, and beauty. But I certainly experienced, quite distinctly, those feelings of frustration and powerlessness as I watched what was happening in my world.

I remember, for example, how I felt when I observed the trend of shops and banks and department stores ripping out hand-planed mahogany and replacing it with blond pine or even synthetic tile. My mother would do most

of her shopping on Saturdays, and I would accompany her through downtown Great Falls. It was like a dagger through my heart to watch the "renovating" and "remodeling" (or, as I came to think of it later, the remuddling) of downtown Great Falls. You might think "dagger in the heart" is an extreme sentiment for a young boy, but I believe things are more painful to us when we feel powerless, and especially when no one else seems to share those feelings. Today, of course, people "ooh" and "aah" over hand-carved mahogany and walnut, exclaim over the artistry of Victorian craftsmen, and pay tremendous sums to have this type of work replicated. But in the 1950s, and especially in Montana, there were very few people with whom a young boy with these sensibilities could communicate about such matters. My mother, however, was one.

I never knew my father, but I was extremely close to my mother, Myrtle Deem Ellingsen. She was a good mother, a good friend, and a good companion. My bond with her made up, at least in part, for the fact that I was in most ways quite a loner. In fact, throughout my entire childhood and adolescence, I really only had one close friend—a ranch kid named Gregg Carlson. It's not that I didn't like other children. I was friendly with them, and they were kind to me. But we didn't seem to have much to talk about. I was not particularly interested in sports, and as I got older, I was too shy to be distracted by girls. I naturally gravitated to older people, to people with stories to tell. Perhaps even more, I gravitated to the graceful old buildings of the Victorian era.

McKinley School, for example, where I attended grade school, was a majestically constructed old building from the turn of the 20th century. That is where, in third grade, I learned the graceful and flowing lines of Spencerian script—a skill that would later stand me in good stead on many occasions.

The secondary school I attended—Paris Gibson High School—was another impeccably constructed building that had an influence on me. It was built like a mighty castle, designed to withstand the ages, with walls of huge stone blocks, stair steps of full logs, and beautiful golden oak woodwork.

It was quite early in my childhood that I was introduced to a different type of building style, in a different type of setting. This experience was to have a profound and lifelong impact on me, introducing me both to the architecture of the early West and to the idea of preservation. What I am referring to is "Old Town," the brilliant creation of the man who, many years later, was to become my mentor: Charles A. Bovey.

Old Town was, essentially, a collection of old Montana buildings that Charlie had acquired, starting with the Sullivan Saddlery from Fort Benton. The saddlery had been one of the haunts

Charlie Bovey's "OLD TOWN"

of the painter Charlie Russell, and Charlie Bovey felt it should be preserved. He had it trucked to the exhibit hall of the Great Falls fairground in 1941, and other buildings soon followed. Charlie then arranged the buildings (all of which had to be reassembled) as they might have originally appeared. His intent was to create the atmosphere of a typical Montana street in the 1800s. From the perspective of one very small boy, at least, it was a wild success.

Old Town, for me, opened a window to the past, and my first clear memory is from that wonderful place. I was so small I could barely walk, and yet I remember distinctly the player piano (which now resides in Nevada City—it's the one with the birds on the glass). That player piano seemed like a magical object to me, beckoning me to step into another era. Even today, player pianos affect me in that same way. As I grew older, we made countless trips to Old Town. More than anything, I believe,

Charlie Bovey's Old Town, circa 1942. What made Old Town unique was the use of original buildings — and people loved it!

THE FAIRWEATHER INN

The lot on which the Fairweather Inn was built was one of the first preemptions of land in Virginia City. It was deeded from the Virginia Town Co., Henry Edgar, Vice President, to J. D. Lomax and John Pitilla on September 18, 1863, for the sum of $150. The building sold, in 1866, for $2,500. At this time, it was occupied by Rosenbaum and Shoumaker, butchers, and was called The Metropolitan Meat Market.

The building seems to have been converted from a meat market to a hotel and saloon in the 1880s. It was acquired in 1896 by Frank McKeen, at which time it was described as a "saloon and fittings." McKeen was a colorful personality who, prepared for any eventuality in life, kept a casket in the basement. He named his place The Anaconda Hotel, and it had both a dining room and a bar. The hotel was sold in 1935 to Humphrey's Gold Corporation, and, in 1946, to Charlie Bovey.

Charlie and Sue found the Anaconda to be a rather unappealing structure. They decided to remodel it, copying the style of Montana's first hotel—The Goodrich House—in Bannack. The ceilings were lowered to nine feet, and the roof on the west side was raised slightly in order to form a second floor.

The Fairweather Inn is, of course, named after Bill Fairweather, the discoverer of gold in Alder Gulch.

those visits made me realize that I was not completely alone in treasuring old buildings and old objects, which I came to feel were almost like emissaries from the past.

When I was somewhat older, my mother and I, along with her sister, Alta Deem, made our first trip to Virginia City and Nevada City. That was in 1952. On our second trip, in 1956, I was better able to appreciate what I was seeing. We rode the train from Great Falls to Helena (an adventure in itself) and then on to Butte. Between Helena and Butte we rode in the observation car. What a spectacular ride! What a shame that one can no longer travel in that style around our state.

We arrived at the Great Northern Depot in Butte and took a room at the Finlen Hotel, which I found to be impressive and elegant. The next morning, after breakfast, we continued our journey with what was (somewhat misleadingly) called the Northern Pacific Transport Stage. It was, in reality, a rather homely vehicle, half-bus, half-truck, smelling of oily smoke, with a cargo of twittering baby chicks, and powered by a noisy, rattling engine. I thought it was magnificent.

My excitement overcame my motion sickness, and as we wound our way through the thick forest of Douglas fir and lodgepole pine, past formations of granite that looked like they had been deposited there by a giant, over the Continental Divide and into the Ruby Valley, I imagined I was riding an old-time stage. I will still in that frame of mind when, later that afternoon, we finally arrived in Virginia City. We booked a room at the Fairweather Inn, and then I set out immediately to explore. My impressions from that day are still crystal clear. I remember the quality of the light, and the shadows on the mountains around Alder Gulch, and the pleasant dustiness of the side streets. I remember the buildings, each of them with different architectural details, or in some cases, quite different styles, but all of them somehow making a harmonious whole. I was fascinated by the building that housed the *Montana Post*, Montana's first newspaper. I couldn't take my eyes off the old-fashioned equipment, especially the printing press. Even though I didn't know exactly the use of every piece of machinery, I was mesmerized by the brass and iron and steel, by the cogs and wheels and gears, and I understood, with a flash of insight, that

what I was looking at represented the pinnacle of technology of another era. I understood even then that the main value of technology, apart from whatever practical application a particular piece of equipment or machinery might offer, is that it is a manifestation of human ingenuity; and I understood that human ingenuity is the same from generation to generation, and from era to era.

More than anything, I remember that trip to Virginia City because I felt like I had come home. Even though I was young and very shy, and had not yet seen much of the world, I felt this was my place, that it was a place I had a right to be.

Old Town, for me, was a wonderful sort of museum, a way to stimulate my imagination. Virginia City and Nevada City, on the other hand, seemed like real life. On the streets of Virginia City, I felt I was not merely imagining the past—I was in the past. That feeling stayed with me for the entire trip back to Great Falls. I was nine years old.

We made more trips to Virginia City, and of course, countless visits to Old Town. I also enjoyed our

This beautiful Great Falls Victorian was torn down unceremoniously. The author, at age 12, made this drawing from memory.

excursions to Helena, a city with many beautiful buildings (this was before the tragedy of urban renewal), and to Butte. Those were the happiest times of my childhood. I spent hours studying these buildings, admiring them, and, in a sense, trying to learn their language.

When I was in first grade, my teacher thought I was color blind, because when the class colored with crayons, I only used black and brown. My drawings back then were typically of pot-bellied stoves, stove pipes, Monarch ranges, and the like. And—always—drawings of old buildings.

My interests broadened, naturally, as I grew older. I came to understand more of world history and world politics, and I tried to read as widely as I could. My reading deepened my knowledge of other cultures, historical periods, and architectural styles. And it also deepened my appreciation for my beloved Victorian architecture and enabled me to understand it in historical context. I would love to have become an architect, but as a high school student, I found no one to encourage me in that pursuit. On the contrary, my teachers and counselors thought I was being impractical and unwise. One teacher lent a sympathetic ear until I confessed my chief interest and inspiration derived from the building styles of the Victorian period.

"You'll never get a job," he told me. "You'll only be miserable. Go into another field."

I heard that advice over and over, but I was never completely swayed by it. I enrolled at Montana State University in Bozeman and majored in industrial arts, with a minor in history. After graduating, I was accepted into a graduate program in history and earned a master's degree in that discipline with a minor in architecture and archeology. At MSU, although most people still pooh-poohed the idea of studying Victorian architecture, I did find two professors who shared my enthusiasm and who encouraged me. One of them was Dr. Mike Malone, who was my graduate advisor and who later became president of the university. The other was Professor John De Haas, who taught the history of architecture. He had an immeasurable influence on my view of history and preservation. When I first became acquainted with him, his eyesight was failing, and later he hired me to drive him and be his guide. What was a terrible tragedy for this brilliant man—his rapidly failing eyesight—was a blessing for me because it allowed me to spend hours with him, absorbing his knowledge and his philosophy. Professor De Haas gave me a deeper understanding of early Montana architecture and its connection to Montana history. He co-founded the Montana Ghost Town Preservation Society. Perhaps more than anyone else at that time, John De Haas was a champion for the study, preservation, and documentation of Montana's old mining communities and ghost towns. It was he who made me understand why preservation matters. And it was he, more than anyone, who prepared me for the next turn in my life's path—one that would lead me to Virginia City and to Charlie Bovey.

MUSIC MACHINES AND THE BALE OF HAY

As I have described elsewhere in these pages, I have had a life-long fascination with the music machines that you can see in the Bale of Hay Saloon. This famous building was occupied from 1869 to about 1890 by J. F. Stoer, a merchant in groceries and alcoholic spirits. The building was then turned into a saloon by Messrs. Smith and Boyd, who dubbed it "The Bale of Hay." Smith and Boyd stayed in business until about 1908. It then stood empty until 1945, at which time it was restored by Charlie Bovey. The main part of "The Bale" is exactly as it was when Charlie found it, except for the ornate 1880-vintage bar and back bar, which were brought from Benchland, Montana.

The old Bale of Hay was a magical place, a sort of trip in time into that vanished, pre-Prohibition Old West. The front room

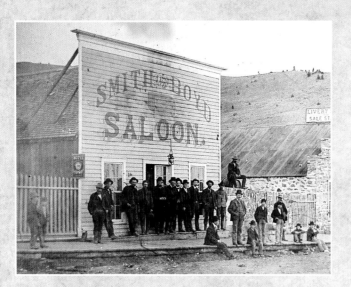

was the player piano museum, where even young kids were welcome: a dozen orchestrions, various arcade machines, a long line of cast-iron mutoscopes, and, at one time, a haunting gypsy fortuneteller in her case. Behind swinging doors was the bar room—he back bar of magnificent, Eastlake-style walnut, glittered with beveled mirrors; the front bar, worn smooth over the years by the elbows and forearms of a wide assortment of humanity. And then there was a sort of "inner Sanctum," a couple of dark rooms with elaborate reddish wallpaper, gold wainscoting, oversize nude paintings, and the melancholy strains of the Reproduco Pipe Organ.

It could be argued that no authentic Old West saloon would have so many player pianos, but then, the Bale was in many ways more like a strange and pleasant dream than a "re-creation." It had an almost indescribable realism that no museum could approach.

Charlie Bovey's collection of rare music machines grew, and people marveled at the orchestrions in the Bale of Hay, the double violin player at the Wells Fargo Coffee House, the soft music boxes in the hotels, and the ear-splitting marches of the gigantic band organs in the Nevada City Music Hall.

A fire on Friday the 13th, 1983, badly burned many of the precious music machines. Some were beautifully restored in other parts of the world. But I will always remember the sounds they made—melodic and cacophonous, harsh and sweet—like ghosts from the past.

TRAVELS WITH CHARLIE

REFLECTIONS ON MY YEARS AS AN EMPLOYEE AND COMPANION
OF CHARLES ARGALIS BOVEY.

WITH SOME INSIGHT INTO THE LIFE OF THIS REMARKABLE MAN,
BASED ON A LARGE NUMBER OF CONVERSATIONS WITH HIM, AS WELL
AS INFORMATION GLEANED FROM OTHER SOURCES

From the time I was a child in Great Falls, visiting Old Town with my mother, the world view of Charles A. Bovey helped shape my life. Today, 33 years after his death, his philosophy and personality still exert an influence on me.

Charlie Bovey was an extraordinary man of great vision, and it is perhaps difficult to appreciate from a modern perspective the impact he had on attitudes toward the preservation of historic buildings in the American West. Despite his remarkable legacy, it is extraordinary how little has been written about Charlie Bovey and how little is known about him. And yet, without his vision and perseverance, it is quite possible that very few of the historic buildings that delight today's visitor to Virginia City would still be standing.

Today, we are fortunate to have throughout the western United States many historic preservation societies, foundations, and organizations, all of them doing important work. In particular, I have to mention the National Trust for Historic Preservation for the work it has carried out nationally and in many western states, including Montana. Here in our own state, in addition to the wonderful resources provided by the Montana Historical Society, we have the Montana Preservation Alliance, the Montana History Foundation, and other local groups too numerous to mention. All of these organizations identify buildings, communities, and artifacts of historic value, and work diligently to preserve, restore, and document them. What is perhaps most encouraging is that, increasingly, these organizations have been finding innovative ways to collaborate. For someone passionate about the history of the West, as I am, it is wonderful to be living in this era in which so many resources are devoted to historic preservation. It was not always thus.

At the time Charlie Bovey first started to carry out what became his life's work, the intrinsic importance of historic preservation in the West was not at all taken for granted. In fact, Charlie's passion for old buildings and artifacts was viewed by many as rather eccentric, to say the least. But he was a man who was undeterred by other people's opinions of what was and was not appropriate, seemly, or fashionable. He was driven his entire life by an inner fire, one that drew him steadily away from the life of power and high society he was born to, and toward the West.

Charles Argalis Bovey was born in May 1907 in Minneapolis, Minnesota, and was one of the heirs to the Washburn Crosby Milling Corporation, later known as General Mills. As a child and young man, he had all the advantages that wealth and social status confer, including international travel and the best educational opportunities. At the age of 16, he was sent to Andover, Massachusetts, to attend the well-regarded Phillips Academy. But, by Charlie's own admission, he was a less-than-model student. In fact, as he told me, he often found school to be downright boring and irrelevant.

When it came time for him to attend an Ivy League college (as was expected of someone of his social standing), he and his father had a man-to-man talk, at the conclusion of which it became clear that four expensive years at Yale, for this particular young man, would be a waste of time, money, and effort. It was decided instead that Charlie would forego higher education and immediately enter the family business.

To the credit of Bovey, Sr., he didn't immediately place his 19-year-old son in a position of status. Instead, he shipped Charlie off to the hinterlands—Great Falls, Montana—to work in a flour mill and learn the business from the ground up. He arrived with $200 in his pocket, which was to be his allowance for the year, and a letter of introduction to the manager of the mill. The manager handed Charlie a broom and told him to start sweeping the floor.

Flour milling turned out to be as little to Charlie's liking as school was. He made an effort to learn the business, but his interests lay elsewhere. He had always yearned to come to the West, and now that he was here he was captivated by the wide-open,

SAUERBIER BLACKSMITH SHOP

A saloon and dance hall were supposed to have been the original occupants of this 1863-vintage building. By the late 1860s, however, it had been converted into a blacksmith shop. The hand-crafted French doors with their transoms and the remnants of a few dentils still clinging to the cornice recall its dance hall era. Inside, one can note a still older cabin in the rear, probably one of the first crude shelters built in June 1863. Various features have been added over the years, writing the structure's history in boards, nails, and labor.

Neither the interior nor the exterior of the building have changed since it was acquired by Charlie Bovey from the Sauerbier family, who operated it from 1882 until the 1930s. The original equipment, including the forge, anvil, tire shrinker, bellows, drill press, and unique skylight, are still in place—exactly as they were left on the last day of business.

Charles F. Sauerbier moved to Virginia City in 1882, after two years in Adobetown (just down the gulch from Nevada City.) He worked on stagecoaches, and shod the teams of oxen that brought much-needed goods into the region via either Corinne, Utah, or Fort Benton, Montana. Charles Sauerbier was succeeded by his son, Karl, who was born in Virginia City in 1889 and lived there his entire life. He built a home, which still stands today behind the shop, from logs taken from the first jail in Virginia City.

Charles Argalis
Bovey, 1977

dramatic landscape in which he found himself. He loved looking at the Front Range of the Rocky Mountains and the island ranges of central Montana; he loved the Missouri River that wound through Great Falls; he loved the rolling countryside where fields of wheat and barley alternated with cattle ranches. Not too many years passed before the idea of being a rancher took hold of him, and (with considerable difficulty) he convinced his father that his future lay in cattle rather than flour milling. His father felt Charlie was giving up his chances of success in life by becoming "a common, ordinary rancher." At that point, however, Charlie had enough of his own money to proceed with his plan, so his father had to relent. At the same time, Charlie had started seeing a beautiful young third-generation Montana woman named Rachel Sue Ford, whose father was president of the Great Falls National Bank. This turned out to be fortuitous, as Mr. Ford's bank had foreclosed on a number of local agricultural properties. One of them was east of Great Falls, and that was to become the first of Charlie Bovey's ranches. He later acquired a sheep ranch and raised wheat as well.

 Sue Ford Bovey

Charlie and Sue were married in 1933, by which time he was ranching full time. And he wasn't living the life of a gentleman rancher or "hobby rancher." Charlie was a hard worker who didn't shy away from physical tasks, and he took his ranching career seriously. Though he worked long hours, he still had ample opportunity to explore his surroundings, and it was not only the landscape that caught Charlie's attention. He was enthralled by the old buildings he saw everywhere: rough herder's quarters, bunkhouses, and ranch houses in the country, and more refined building styles in the towns. Even in the 1920s, these older buildings were being neglected and sometimes torn down in favor of more modern styles. Charlie and Sue both had a passion for western history, and each must have recognized in the other a kindred spirit. They would take long drives through the Montana countryside, Sue reading aloud from books on Montana history. On these forays they began collecting in earnest. At first they acquired smaller items: books, paintings, furniture, musical instruments, farm implements and tools, vintage clothing, Victorian knick-knacks. It wasn't long, however, before Charlie started putting significant energy, time, and resources into the restoration and preservation of old buildings. I described earlier how he had moved the Sullivan Saddlery from Fort Benton. That was only the beginning of the activity that would become his life's work.

While Charlie's Minnesota family was somewhat dismayed at his life choices, in Montana he had become an individual of significant influence and social standing. (Of course, his marriage to Rachel Sue Ford certainly didn't hurt!) In 1942 Charles Bovey was elected to the Montana House of Representatives, as a Democrat representing Cascade County. He was elected to a second term, and subsequently served as a state senator from Cascade County until 1965. While in office, he

was an eloquent advocate for the rights of the mentally ill. He also, of course, worked tirelessly to make the public aware of the importance of preserving the buildings and communities that he felt were the embodiment of Montana's history.

It was two years after Charlie was first elected that he and Sue made their first visit to Virginia City. They had heard that there were old historic buildings there in need of restoration, but they weren't quite prepared for what they found when they drove over the pass from Ennis, along a rutted dirt road, through the open landscape of high sagebrush bowls fringed with juniper, and down into Alder Gulch. Charlie told me that as soon as they entered Virginia City, he realized simultaneously that the place was a national treasure, and that many of the buildings had been seriously neglected and were in danger of being destroyed.

Charlie and Sue both understood that Virginia City presented a unique opportunity to preserve an entire town with enormous significance in

western history. They also understood that time was of the essence. In fact, even on that first visit, they witnessed boards being pulled from old buildings for firewood or for scrap lumber. At that time, Virginia City had a population of around 400 souls, some of them still engaged in mining, while others had small businesses of various kinds. The town, however, like many small western communities, was barely hanging on, with an economy on life support.

Immediately after that first visit, with the help of historian Joseph Kinsey Howard and other concerned citizens, Charlie helped found the Historic Landmark Society of Montana, an organization that was intended to call attention to and preserve historically important buildings and landmarks in Montana. The membership quickly rose to about 400, a not insignificant number, and enthusiasm for the mission of the Society was high.

 The existing Dance and Stuart Store is an exact copy of the original – shown here in 1910 – in every detail.

Before the Boveys
began their restoration
efforts, this is what
a tourist might have
seen in Virginia City.

THE MONTANA POST

The Montana Post was the first newspaper of Montana Territory, and was for a time hugely influential among the citizenry of Alder Gulch and far beyond. It was founded on August 27, 1864, by J. Buchanan, who sold it after only two issues to D. W. Tilton & Co.

By the time the Post was ready to print its third issue, the paper had a new editor—the illustrious Professor Thomas Dimsdale. About a year after taking the reins of the Post, Dimsdale began to publish, in serial form, his "Vigilantes of Montana," which was to become the first book printed in Montana.

The stone print shop of the Montana Post was completed on January 10, 1865. Prior to that the paper had been published in a log building on Idaho Street. On September 22, 1866, the Montana Post building was graced with a new storefront and sign. Ironically, Professor Dimsdale died on the same day.

In 1868, joining the restless stream of Alder Gulch citizens and businesses, the Montana Post moved its operations to Helena. It suspended publication in the spring of 1869.

In the building where the Post had originated in Virginia City, D. W. Tilton continued to operate his City Book Store for many years.

After 1900, the City Book Store corner became the saloon of the adjacent Virginia (or Idaho or International) Hotel. In 1937 the Montana Post, along with the Virginia Hotel, burned to the ground.

In 1946 the Historic Landmark Society of Montana, with funds donated by Charlie Bovey, began the reconstruction of the building. The stone walls of the print shop remained, and after extensive research, the frame store was reconstructed exactly as it had been and furnished with authentic period printing equipment and type.

The members gave serious thought to what communities they should concentrate on first and gave consideration to the Saint Peter's Mission, Bannack, Fort Logan, and other locations. Some of the first projects included restoration of an old fur trader's cabin near Fort Benton, a mill near Craig, and the jail at Bannack. In Virginia City, the Society bought and completely restored the building—almost completely destroyed—that had once housed Montana's first newspaper—the *Montana Post*.

Charlie was a major contributor (in fact, the primary contributor) to the Society. In many cases, not being a particularly patient man, he found it simpler to buy the buildings himself. As time went by, he (and the Historic Landmark Society of Montana) concentrated his energies and resources on Alder Gulch. And that, in a word, is how Charles A. Bovey soon acquired a significant number of the important buildings of Virginia City. For his first acquisition, in 1944, he told me he paid the sum of $100. In 1945 he bought the Judge Blake House on Idaho Street. The next year he began acquiring commercial buildings, including the Buford Store and others. Word quickly spread

in Madison County that an eccentric fellow with deep pockets had fallen in love with Virginia City, and he was in a buying mood. It wasn't long before Charlie found himself the owner of more than 100 buildings in Alder Gulch, including the Bale of Hay Saloon, the Hangman's Building, the Gilbert house and brewery, and others. The question facing him was: Now that he owned a significant number of the oldest structures in the most historically important community in Montana, what was he going to do with them?

Although Charlie was a man of means, he was also a man who liked to roll up his sleeves and do physical labor. In part, no doubt, this was because he didn't want to give the impression that he thought he was better than anyone else. In part it was because he was famously frugal and didn't want to pay someone to perform work that he could do himself. But mostly, Charlie believed—as do I—that there is a kind of profound knowledge to be gained by physical work, especially when that work involves the restoration of buildings from another time. It is hardly an exaggeration to say that Charlie was acquainted with every board, beam, shingle, stone, brick, nail, and dowel in Alder Gulch.

It was an interesting time in Virginia City. Elsewhere in the United States, WWII had helped our recovery from the Great Depression. In Virginia City, however (and doubtless in many towns of similar size across the nation), the war actually accelerated the community's decline, with many of the men joining the service, and their families often moving away to larger towns to seek work. The Grant Mine, on the edge of Virginia City, still employed a few dozen men, and that was essentially what kept the community alive. The other main source of revenue, though by no means a large one, was tourism. It was in the latter that Charlie saw Virginia City's future.

The word "tourism," for a historic preservationist, can have mixed connotations. Charlie was certainly a preservationist, and a serious one, but he was also a pragmatist. He saw in tourism a way to bring income to Virginia City and keep the community vibrant, and as a way to help restore and maintain the precious buildings he was only beginning to inventory. Perhaps most important of all, he wanted to bring people to Virginia City because he recognized the historical significance

of the town, and he badly wanted other people to see in this remarkable collection of buildings the same value that he did.

In 1945, Charlie began the Herculean task of restoring his Virginia City properties. He didn't go about this haphazardly. He understood what each of the buildings represented, and he took great pains not simply to restore them, but to do so in a way that captured the feel of the period in which they had been built. It was Charlie's intention from the beginning to create a kind of museum: not the "look-but-don't-touch" variety, but a kind of museum that lived and breathed and invited visitors to step into the past. To help create what he considered an authentic atmosphere, Charlie began to fill the buildings with various antiques, artifacts, tools, and clothing he had collected from around the western United States, but primarily Montana.

The next step for Charlie and Sue was to begin opening businesses in some of the historic buildings. They wanted to make sure that visitors had somewhere to eat, somewhere to sleep, and something to amuse them. In the span of a few short years, Charlie opened a number of businesses, including the Wells Fargo Coffee House in the Buford Block, the Bale of Hay Saloon, the Fairweather Inn, and others. He took what had been the Smith and Boyd Livery Stable and turned it into a performing venue for The Virginia City Players. It wasn't long before many more businesses had sprung up in our historic streets. Where Virginia City had once been sleepy and almost moribund, it was now, in the summer season at least, thriving. Restaurants and hotels were staffed by dozens of young people—mostly college students—from around the state. There were music machines and wagon rides and reenactments and theater performances. Charlie wanted there to be something for everybody, but this was not entertainment that catered to the lowest common denominator. People from all over Montana—indeed, from all over the world—came to visit. Some of them were scholars of western history, but most came because they believed Virginia City could give them an authentic experience, a true taste of the Old West. Many of these visitors returned year after year, and they always went away happy. And if they were happy, then so was

 A poster for The Virginia City Players, produced by the author

A CHRISTMAS CARD
TO MR. BOVEY

It was the summer before my sophomore year in high school, on our annual visit to Virginia City, when I did this drawing of the toy store, a place that had always captured my imagination. The original is 8½" x 11", the size I have always used for most of my drawings.

My mother sent the drawing to a place back East somewhere called Ray's Photo Service, and had 4" x 5" cards printed on good-quality cardstock. We used the toy store cards as our Christmas cards that year, but I had really done the drawing for Charlie Bovey. At the time, I didn't know Charlie very well, but I felt the need to give him something, and resolved to deliver his card to him in person.

I wrote a Christmas greeting on the card, walked down to the Bovey residence at 401 4th Avenue North in Great Falls, and, screwing up my courage, rang the bell. A car was parked in the driveway, so I knew they were home. When nobody answered, I walked downtown, figuring Sue was probably shopping for furs or diamonds at The Paris, the fancy department store in Great Falls. Not finding her or Charlie there, I returned to their house and rang the bell again. Finally, somewhat disappointed, I put the card in the letter slot.

I later learned that when they were in the Great Falls area, Charlie and Sue stayed at their ranch, and that they only left a car parked at the house to discourage intruders. I also learned that both Charlie and Sue were much more likely to be found at a lumber yard than at a department store.

The next summer, in Virginia City, Charlie thanked me for the card. Many years later, after Charlie and Sue had both passed away, the bank that managed the Bovey estate asked me to go to their ranch house to help get their affairs in order. I walked through the house, taking inventory. In the bedroom, I saw a card placed prominently in the frame of the mirror. It was the card I had given Charlie.

Charlie Bovey. The eccentric and stubborn Minneapolis milling heir, legislator, rancher, and collector had finally found his calling. It was many years later, when my life's path intersected with Charlie, that I found my own calling. This is how it came about.

My mother and I, as I have related earlier, made annual "pilgrimages" to Virginia City. As a child, these trips were the high point of my life. I never tired of the music machines, or the museum with the petrified cat and the foot of "Clubfoot George" under a glass dome. Most of all, I enjoyed simply wandering the streets and trying to decipher and absorb what the buildings had to teach me.

From the time I was seven or eight, I knew who Charlie Bovey was. He was a larger-than-life character in Virginia City. I finally met him when I was 14 years old, and I have to believe he saw in me a kindred spirit. When he perceived how deeply I was interested in historic preservation, he handed me a set of keys that opened virtually every building in Virginia City, and told me to sketch and

photograph to my heart's content. After that, I talked to Charlie every time we visited, and I perceived that he began to take me seriously, young though I was, as a historian and preservationist-in-the-making. We kept in touch throughout the time I was at Montana State University. Shortly after receiving my graduate degree, I ran into Charlie one day at the Bale of Hay Saloon, and out of the blue, he asked me to come to work for him as a curator as soon as my other obligations were fulfilled. I was flattered by the proposal, but there were two immediate obstacles in the way. The first was a previous offer of employment by the Bureau of Land Management. I had worked the year before for the BLM, supervising restoration work in the Montana ghost town of Garnet, and had found it to be very fulfilling work. The pay—for a young man in 1971—was a respectable if not overwhelming $40 per day.

The second obstacle had to do with a commitment to serve in the U.S. Army! I reported to Fort Belvoir in Virginia that fall, but much to my relief, with the war in Viet Nam winding down, I was released in February 1972. Immediately after my release, Charlie pre-empted the BLM by taking me to lunch and repeating his offer of work for him—at half of the BLM salary. Naturally I jumped at the chance.

Thus began my formal relationship with Charlie Bovey. From 1972, up to the time of Charlie's passing in 1978, I spent nearly every day working with him. It was an educational, occasionally frustrating, and absolutely wonderful six years. To say Charlie was a frugal man would be somewhat of an understatement. He always drove a used car. He was a notoriously bad tipper. And although he was willing to spend freely when it was a question of buying a building or artifact, he seemed unable to put a monetary value on other people's labor. Personally, I could not have cared less. I felt that the opportunity to live in Nevada City (where I acquired a house) and perform restoration work on historic buildings was priceless.

By the time I began working with Charlie, the work on Virginia City was, for all intents and purposes, complete. Charlie and I focused much of our attention on the restoration or, rather,

re-creation of Nevada City. And what a wonderful undertaking that was! While Virginia City is unique in having so many original and intact buildings, Nevada City is more of a work of historical fiction. A visitor to Nevada City might not realize where the buildings came from or how much work was involved in moving and re-erecting them. Having assisted with much of this project, I can tell you the effort and planning to carry it out was considerable.

At this point I would like to add a few words about Nevada City. The history of this little community is a fascinating one, and in fact, I intend to write a book about it in the future. For now, however, I will limit myself to the following brief sketch.

At the height of the gold rush, Nevada City was (after Virginia City) the second most important community of Alder Gulch. It was here, in 1863, that George Ives was hanged for murder, an event that would lead to the Vigilante hangings in the weeks to follow. At its height, Nevada City had dozens of stores, shops, livery stables, lodging houses, eateries, and other business. For a short

time, it was quite a bustling place. Within a few short years, however, the population had fallen to under a hundred souls. By the mid-1870s, only ten years after being settled, Nevada City had for all intents and purposes become a ghost town.

Many of the buildings here—in contrast to Virginia City—were destroyed. The home of Nevada City's last residents, the Finney family, was still standing when Charlie Bovey arrived. Along with several neighboring houses, the Finney place was the core around which Charlie began to rebuild Nevada City. Some of the first "new" buildings were those Charlie moved from Old Town in Great Falls, starting in 1959. A few of those were originally from Alder Gulch, but most—like the Sullivan Saddlery—were from elsewhere in Montana. In fact, Nevada City is in many respects like Old Town

 Sullivan Saddlery and Elkhorn barbershop – two of the first buildings reassembled in Nevada City

NEVADA CITY ♡H MONTANA

John A. Ellingsen DECEMBER 5, 1988

used to be, except that it is in a more natural setting. Like Old Town, it represents equal parts history and fiction, with the same intent of helping visitors imagine the past. By the time I had begun working with Charlie, he was scouring the remotest corners of Madison County for buildings that were historically and stylistically appropriate for Nevada City. That is not to say they needed to be from a specific historical period, but as Charlie explained to me, they needed to have a certain "feel" to them. In order to find these buildings, we spent countless hours and days driving back roads,

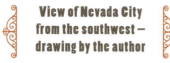
View of Nevada City from the southwest – drawing by the author

them were fascinating to us. We found them around the edges of the Tobacco Root Mountains, the Ruby Range, the Madison Range, and the Gravelly Range. Every one of these excursions, for me, was like a treasure hunt. We would hear a rumor of a building, and off we would go, never knowing what we would find. Many of these trips, naturally, turned out to be wild goose chases. We might not be able to agree on a price with the owner; or the building in question might be too modern, or too dilapidated to be worth repairing, or for some reason devoid of that "feel" we were seeking. However, most of the time, our efforts resulted in success. Charlie and I would be giddy on our drive home, planning how to move the building and where to erect it. Not even my employer's infernal habit of chain smoking with the windows rolled up, nearly suffocating me with secondhand smoke, could dampen my excitement.

In some cases, we could move the buildings whole, but often we had to dismantle them almost completely. This required, of course, careful measuring and planning. I sketched and measured each of these buildings, and we numbered the logs

hiking, knocking on doors. We talked to ranchers and farmers, old miners, local historians, merchants, and anyone who might know where an old building might be for sale. Many of these were rough cabins of cottonwood or fir logs; some were outbuildings; some were sheds or barns. All of

and boards before taking them apart. Although most of them were architecturally simple—even somewhat crude—they displayed a real ingenuity on the part of their builders, for they were constructed from scratch out of the materials at hand. Logs had to be cut and fitted, boards had to be sawn and planed, dowels had to be carved and shakes split with simple hand tools. Many of these older buildings—most, in fact—were constructed without the aid of nails or other fasteners. To have been able to assist in the reconstruction of so many historic buildings of this type afforded me a priceless education in the vernacular western architecture of the 1800s.

All good things, they say, must come to an end, and so did my time with Charlie. He had a heart murmur—something that had kept him out of WWII and occasionally troubled him, his rugged appearance notwithstanding. His smoking habit, of course, made things worse. As far as I could tell,

however, his health was fine on the morning of June 9, 1978, when he knocked on my door and invited me to breakfast. It was a beautiful morning, with blue sky and cool, still air. We went to the Virginia City Café, and we both ordered pancakes, as we often did. Though Charlie had offered to buy me breakfast, he forgot his wallet, as was often the case, so I paid for both of us.

Later that morning, I was working at home, when I heard Sue Bovey yelling: "Charlie's having a heart attack!"

By the time I got to him, there was nothing to be done. I held his hand and heard myself saying the Lord's Prayer.

"Take care of things," he told me. Those were the last words to pass the lips of Charles Argalis Bovey, a great Montanan, and a great man.

FROM TRAGEDY TO TRIUMPH

A BRIEF SYNOPSIS OF THE DRAMATIC SAVING OF
VIRGINIA CITY AND NEVADA CITY,

FROM THE PERSPECTIVE OF ONE WHO WAS AT FIRST
NAÏVE ABOUT THE POLITICAL PROCESS, BUT WHO CONTRIBUTED
IN A MODEST WAY TO THIS CRUCIAL EFFORT

The death of Charlie Bovey was a terrible blow to me. I never knew my own father, and in many ways, Charlie had filled that role in my life. The hours and days after his death were a blur to me. I remember the ambulance arriving, and people coming and going, and not much more. I found a quiet room where I could be by myself and cried. From one day to the next, my life had changed.

More than 200 mourners came to Charlie's service, most of them people I didn't know. The wild iris was in bloom, and the flax, and we made bouquets with native wildflowers. Charlie was buried in Great Falls, and I was one of the pallbearers. I also spoke at the funeral, though I felt somewhat out of place.

Afterwards, there was a reception at the Bovey house at 401 4th Avenue North in Great Falls. Ford Bovey, Charlie's son, approached me and asked me to continue to work for the family. At that point, Virginia City was my life, and I couldn't imagine doing anything else. Naturally I said yes.

Charlie's death was a shock: not only to me personally, but to the community of Virginia City, and to everyone who cared about it. For many of us, Charlie and his larger-than-life personality had become synonymous with Virginia City. It was his vision that had saved the place from oblivion; his vision that had put it back on the map; and his vision, or so I had always assumed, that would guide it into the future. His sudden passing changed all that.

Still, life goes on. As the numbness slowly wore off, I got back to the same restoration and preservation work I had carried out before Charlie's death.

The author receives the Governor's Award for Historic Preservation from Montana Governor Marc Racicot, January 1997.

Charlie's widow, Sue, also began to play a more prominent role in the day-to-day running of Virginia City. Sue shared Charlie's vision, and she and I became very close. We had a wonderful collaboration right up to the time of her own passing in October 1988.

The Bovey properties in Alder Gulch—Bovey Restorations—were now in the hands of Ford. He did his best to run the various shops and keep up with the restoration work, but he had inherited a business that was steadily losing money year after year. It soon became clear to him, and to others, that this state of affairs was, in the long run, untenable.

By the spring of 1991, Ford was forced to seriously explore his options, including, reluctantly, the sale of some or all of the 100-plus buildings owned by Bovey Restorations. The possibility that Virginia City might be sold and lost raised concerns among preservation and historical organizations, as well as concerned individuals in Montana and around the nation.

Many groups devoted enormous amounts of time and resources to the challenge of saving Virginia City; in particular, the National Trust for Historic Preservation's Denver office and the Montana History Foundation. The groups worked hard to find an entity that could take over ownership of Virginia City in order to protect it in perpetuity. An initial plan was to bring Virginia and Nevada Cities under the aegis of the National Park Service. When that didn't come to fruition, an attempt was made to raise enough private money to buy the buildings and businesses owned by Bovey Restorations and manage them as a nonprofit. This was also unsuccessful.

It finally became clear to many of those concerned that the most logical and feasible solution was for the State of Montana to buy the property. Little by little, this solution was attracting supporters, including then-governor Marc Racicot. Still, the path from wish to reality, from "a rather interesting idea" to a successful vote in the legislature, was a long, difficult, and frustrating one. And time was running out. If a way was not found for the state to acquire the Bovey properties, they were certain to be sold, and Montana would lose one of her greatest treasures.

During this entire process, over the course of several years, I was intensely involved with efforts to raise awareness of the plight of Virginia City. On several occasions, when the Montana legislature was in session, I made the trek to Helena, the capital, to try and sway the legislators. But politics and the political process were foreign to me. In my ill-fitting suit and new city haircut, I was distinctly out of my element. I felt that there was a secret language, or perhaps a secret code of conduct, that was known to everyone in the capitol but me. I still remember my first visit to the legislature, when I mistook a group of lobbyists for legislators. (They had suits and name tags, I reasoned. They must be legislators!) On two occasions, I gave testimony. To a person who was once frightened to say anything in public under any circumstance, it was intimidating in the extreme to testify in front of the somber-faced representatives in the Old Supreme Court in the Montana State Capitol building. Despite my nervousness, I have to believe my passion showed through and that I did have an influence on individual legislators. And, naturally, I was not alone. There was a growing group of individuals and organizations working together, and by the legislative session of 1997, the movement to save Virginia City had gained considerable momentum. Karl Ohs, the representative from Madison County (and later lieutenant governor) had introduced House Bill 14, which authorized the State of Montana to purchase the Bovey properties. That bill, however, had been on a tortuous journey through the legislative process, something I was only beginning to understand.

On the night of April 22, 1997, I didn't sleep at all. I finally got out of bed shortly before 5 a.m., dressed, and made the drive to Helena. It was April 23, the last day of the legislative session. There were a number of spectators in the balcony of the Montana House of Representatives. Only three bills remained to be voted on, one of which was House Bill 14. Those who were present that day—representatives of national, state, and local organizations, along with many individuals—were giddy with anticipation, but nervous. As for me, still wearing my uncomfortable suit, but by now not quite so naïve, the tension was almost literally unbearable. This was not an abstract political battle.

Having survived against all odds for 134 years, would the irreplaceable historic buildings of Virginia City be sold off? Would Charlie Bovey's vision, and his 50 years of labor, be wiped out? What about my own quarter century of work in this place, the place that had become my life?

After several agonizing recesses to caucus, House Bill 14 came up for a final vote. It needed 67 votes to pass. We were on pins and needles as the tally board lit up with green and red lights. It looked like it was mostly green, but I held my breath until the result was announced: 81 in favor, 19 opposed. The State of Montana had been authorized to purchase Bovey Restorations. The historic buildings and artifacts of Virginia City and Nevada City had been saved for future generations.

I will always remember that moment: 4:37 p.m., April 23, 1997. I wanted to cry; I wanted to shout at the top of my lungs, but no sound came. I still couldn't believe it. It was a great day, a triumphant day for Montana history.

"We did it, Charlie," I said.

I love the summer season in Virginia City. I love walking these streets I know so well, watching the visitors who come here from around the world, enjoying their enjoyment. Sometimes I sit at the Outlaw Café, or the Star Bakery down the Gulch in Nevada City, and listen to the conversations around me. I get special pleasure from the children who are here for the first time, under the thrall of the magic of this place, for I see myself in them.

I am often called upon to give tours of Alder Gulch, something I will enjoy doing as long as I live. I like to talk about the history of the buildings, and about the chronology of mining in the West, and about the stage from Fort Benton, and about the "women of the evening" and the road agents and the vigilantes. I do my best to bring the Gulch alive for people, although this place probably doesn't need any help from me to come alive. The streets of Virginia City and Nevada City almost literally breathe western history. I can see in peoples' faces that they feel it too. It is wonderful to watch.

And then, as quickly as it began, the season ends. The stream of visitors slows to a trickle and gradually stops altogether.

Our winters in Virginia City are long and hard. The snow comes early at this elevation and lingers long into the spring like an insensitive guest. The streets that were once packed with visitors are now nearly empty, and the howling wind rattles windows and batters walls. But those walls were built of solid Montana stone and hand-hewn Douglas fir. They have withstood winds like that for well over a century and will do so for another century and more.

Those of us who make our homes here have learned to be patient. And indeed, almost before we realize it, the snow has melted, and the air echoes with the call of sandhill cranes passing overhead as they have for millennia. And soon another sound begins to fill the streets: the laughter and amazed cries of children, the next generation to fall under the spell of Virginia City and to hear the call of the past.

ABOUT THE AUTHOR

John D. Ellingsen is a native of Great Falls, Montana. He has a Masters of Arts and Applied Arts degree from Montana State University. He has won numerous awards for his work in historic preservation, including a lifetime achievement award from the Montana Preservation Alliance, the Governor's Award for Historic Preservation, and a "special award for preservation" from the Department of the Interior for his work at Garnet Ghost Town. Since 1972 he has worked as curator in Virginia City. At present, he is curator emeritus. He lives in Nevada City, Montana.

PHOTO CREDITS

All images courtesy of the author except as follows:

Pages 15, 19, 21, 35, 36–37, 44, 53, 57: Montana Historical Society Research Center Photograph Archives, Helena, MT

Pages 6, 49, 76–77, 79, back cover inset: Kenton Rowe, kentonrowephotography.com

Pages 9, 67: Donnie Sexton

Page 54: Garry Wunderwald photo, courtesy of the author

Page 71: Courtesy of the *Great Falls Tribune*